The Case of Mary Gilmore:

The Curiously Strange Yet True Case of Mary Gilmore, the Irish

Girl Accused of Being a Runaway Slave and Captured on the

Reverse Underground Railroad

The Case of Mary Gilmore:

The Curiously Strange Yet True Case of Mary Gilmore, the Irish

Girl Accused of Being a Runaway Slave and Captured on the

Reverse Underground Railroad

By

Isabelle McEwan

S. Books

s.books@mail.com

First Edition: September 2014

Includes public domain newspaper works from The Liberator Newspaper of 1835 and several primary source documents of the day, all cited within the context of this book.

Cover artwork excerpted from a woodcut that appeared in Harper's Weekly on January 30, 1864 with the caption, "Emancipated Slaves White and Colored."

Dedication

To all of my former students who struggled the biography that

worked for them.

This is a true story.

"In the summer of 1835, a slave-holder from Maryland arrested as his fugitive a young woman in Philadelphia. A trial ensued, when it was most conclusively proved that the alleged slave, Mary Gilmore, was the child of poor Irish parents, and had not a drop of African blood in her veins."

--A View of the Action of the Federal Government, 1839

"Almost everybody has heard of the recent case of Mary Gilmore, of Philadelphia, a
perfectly white girl, of Irish parentage, who was taken up and tried as a runaway slave."

--Anti-Slavery Catechism, 1839

"Considering the wonderful ease and expedition with which fugitives may be recovered by law, it would be very strange if mistakes did not sometimes occur. *How* often they occur cannot, of course, be known, and it is only when a claim is *defeated*, that we are made sensible of the exceedingly precarious tenure by which a poor friendless negro at the north holds his personal liberty. A few years since, a girl of the name of Mary Gilmore was arrested in Philadelphia, as a fugitive slave from Maryland. Testimony was not wanting in support of the claim; yet it was most conclusively proved that she was the daughter of poor *Irish* parents—having not a drop of negro blood in her veins—that the father had absconded, and that the mother had died a drunkard in the Philadelphia hospital, and that the infant had been kindly received and *brought up in a colored family*. Hence the attempt to make a slave of her. --The Anti-Slavery Examiner, 1839

"One example, the case of Mary Gilmore, aptly illustrates the social context of race. Abolitionist William Jay related Gilmore's story in his 1838 pamphlet "condition of the Free People of Color." An alleged fugitive slave from Maryland, Gilmore was arrested in Philadelphia. Her parents were impoverished Irish immigrants; her father had abandoned the family, and her mother had died an alcoholic in a Philadelphia hospital. As an infant, Mary had been taken in and raised by a black family, which, according to Jay, explained the attempt to enslave her. Nowhere is any mention made of Mary Gilmore's having any physical characteristics attributed to blacks. Rather, she was part of a black family, was therefore assumed to be black, and thus became a target for kidnapping and enslavement."
--The Two Lives of Sally Miller: A Case of Mistaken Racial Identity in Antebellum New Orleans, by Carol Wilson, 2007, p. 81

Table of Contents

ACKNOWLEDGMENTS

The author would like to thank the following people and institutions, whose support, moral and otherwise, made writing this book possible: Mary Warnement, The Boston Athenaeum, the Massachusetts Historical Society, the National Endownment for the Humanities (NEH).

All the events in this story were retold from primary source documents from the above mentioned institutions, many of which had not been read in over one hundred years, some in packages that had not been opened since they were first bundled. It is a privilege for me to be able to share this brave woman's story with the world.

First Course: A Recipe for Disaster

"How to Build a Fire: Before starting to build a fire, free the grate from ashes. To do this, put on covers, close front and back dampers, and open oven-damper; turn grate, and ashes will fall into the ash receiver. *If these rules are not followed, ashes will fly over the room.*"

-- Boston Cooking School Cook Book by Fannie Merritt Farmer, 1896

Sugar

"Sugar is a crystalline substance, differing from starch by its sweet taste and solubility in cold water."

When sugar is left to cook over a flame for too long it burns to a blackness that renders it unrecognizable as the white crystal it once was.

The confections I made once were prized for their sweetness. Now they're thrown in my face, a face that I do not even recognize as my own.

Like the sugar left to burn on the fire, I am something else. A possession. A fugitive. A slave. White. Black. Mulatto. Quadroon. I am still Mary Gilmore.

I grew up on South Sixth Street on the corner of Spruce in downtown Philadelphia. My father, Jacob Gilmore, was a baker, a confectioner, the best in the whole city. People came from miles around for his breads and cakes.

I remember it was June of my seventeenth year.

I was next door at the blacksmith's when I heard my father yelling at the old black woman, Maria Congo. She had been stealing from our shop for years, ever since I was a small child. Cakes, sweet breads, meat pies, money.

That was how it all began. The day my life slowly melted away from me.

When the riots began, my only friend, Maureen Kelly burst into our shop and dragged me away. I was all covered in flour and seemed even whiter than I was. She wanted to see the commotion over the runaway slave that had been captured. Maureen Kelly, my only friend, didn't always understand just where I was coming from. She was white and Irish, like me, but her parents were not black, like mine were. My father never talked about it, and I'd learned not to ask, still running to town to see the capture of a fugitive slave was not on my list of things to do. But Maureen and I were the best of friends. Everyone always said that we looked like twins. Curly black hair, deep blue eyes, ivory skin with plenty of freckles. When we looked at each other it was like looking in a mirror.

All of the other girls and boys in Philadelphia made fun of me. I was the only white girl in the city with black parents. But Maureen was different from everybody else. Maureen had been my friend since were very young, so I often forgave her for her indiscretions, forgave here when she made silly suggestions like she just had.

Even our birthdays were the same. We were both born on August 25, 1817. When we'd turned seventeen last summer, our fathers who were neighbors, living right next door to each other, had thrown us a big party. Maureen's father was a blacksmith and had made us identical rings out of old spoons and my father, the baker, had made us the most beautiful cake we'd ever seen. This is how we thought it would always be. Best friends forever. Sometimes fate has other plans.

Maureen dragged me all the way into town where a crowd had gathered in front of the jail. There were blacks and whites together making such an uproar that I couldn't make out exactly what was happening.

I saw a lot of my dad's friends shouting and waving posters and a lot of people I didn't recognize some white and some black. Old lady Maria Congo was in the crowd whispering to some high fluting white man, dressed real proper like, who seemed to be involved in the capturing of this poor man somehow. Maria Congo was waggling her crooked finger in my direction, but I couldn't make out what she was saying, why she was pointing at me in the first place, probably because my father had warned her that the next time she stole from us would be the last time she stole from us. He was going to report her to the sheriff if she did it again.

She must not have liked being threatened like that very much, because she'd been stealing from us since I was a baby. Where would she go now to fill her sweet tooth?

The black man at the center of the rioting was silent. His skin color looked a lot like my father's, but my father, Jacob Gilmore, was not a fugitive slave. He was a free man, and a very successful businessman in Philadelphia. Baker and confectioner extraordinaire. A proud member of the Free African Society of Philadelphia. Thank goodness he would never find himself in a position like this.

"He's being taken back to the South," Maureen whispered to me.

The South -- that was where all the runaway slaves came from. They ran to the North in the hopes of being free, but the federal law made it possible for them to be returned, even if they had lived as free men for years and years, even if they'd started families and business. The runaway slaves would do anything to be free, anything at all to escape the cruel slave masters in the South. But so many got caught. Even free men. And it was getting worse every day with more and more people being captured.

So many got taken back to the South. It seemed that almost every day another person was caught and had to prove that he was a free man or be sent back to the land of slavery. The Fugitive Slave Act of 1793 allowed for the states to make their own rulings, still so many times the judge found in favor of the slave holder from the South.

The way that this slave owner's agent was treating this poor black man was disgraceful. Locked up in shackles, a whip on the slave catcher's hip.

Maureen stood gaping wide-eyed at the spectacle. I turned away. It was so very evil. The evil that men do to other men amazed me.

When my mother had been alive, she'd told me that all men were created equal. She'd told me that on the inside, we were all the same color.

One time she'd cut her finger by accident on a broken shard of glass and held it up to show me.

"We all bleed red on the inside," she'd said. She'd wanted so much to believe what she told me. Believe that it made no difference that she and my father were black and that I was white as the driven snow.

Once I'd asked her how this was possible. She'd only laughed and told me that a broken ol' angel had left me on their doorstep.

I'm ashamed to admit that I'd never asked again. I loved Mary and Jacob Gilmore just as they were, as my parents, who'd raised me for as long as I could remember.

My father saw me with Maureen outside of the jail house. He seemed pretty mad at me for being somewhere he clearly thought I shouldn't be.

My father was carrying a large basket of sweet breads and cakes in his arms, which he'd clearly brought for the prisoner. My father was known throughout the city for his sweets and his kindnesses.

He was known as a man of character and integrity, and it did not surprise me one little bit when I saw him march through the angry crowd, straight up to the prisoner and give that big basket of food to the poor man in shackles and chains.

Jacob Gilmore was fearless, afraid of no one and nothing. He lead an honest life and helped others whenever he could, even mean, stealing, lying people like that Maria Congo, who'd stolen from him for going on seventeen years now. Why was she pointing my father out in the crowd now to the slave owner's agent? Surely, she wouldn't try to insinuate that my father was a runaway. Though these days, free men were falsely accused all the time and had no easy time proving their right to their freedom. The Pennsylvania Abolition Society helped out as much as they could, but still it was difficult.

Then my father came straight at me and grabbing my arm with his hand which was covered in flour, he gently plucked me away from Maureen's side.

"Time to go home now," was all he said. All he needed to say. And I was only too glad to go. In truth, scenes like this made me ill, physically ill. How could men treat each other so badly, purely because of the color of their skin? If hate had a color, I wondered what color it might be.

My father and I must have made quite a sight to see. There we were as the white slave catcher was dragging away "his" black slave, and here we were, my father, black, perhaps blacker than the runaway slave, dragging my lily white arm all the way down Sixth Street, reprimanding me all the way.

I should know better than to go to witness something as evil as that, he'd said, not too severely.

I wanted to apologize. Tell him how I went unwittingly. It had all been Maureen's idea. But I was seventeen and stubborn and silent.

Glancing back over my shoulder, I saw that man they'd captured was being beaten now, whipped, flogged into state of submission.

I hadn't understood before, the concept of slave and owner, the difference between black and white. I'd been raised in a house that was color blind.

Maureen stayed behind, she'd met up with some of her other friends, even though she was my only friend, her parents were white, and other girls parents allowed them to go and to play at Maureen's house. These same girls' parents never allowed them to come to my house, even though we ate far better than probably anyone in Philly.

"They don't know what they're missing," my father would always joke.

Starch

"Starch is a white, glistening powder."

It was at about that time that the rioting began in the streets of Philadelphia. There was looting, pillaging, hatred, and ugliness. In placards plastered all over the city, there were warnings to the colored people that slave catchers were in our midst.

Because of the federal laws that were in place, runaway slaves could be returned to their masters. No man, woman or child of color was safe. Anyone who was black could be accused of being a runaway slave and face charges. The blacks in the North were not safe -- not even the free men like my father.

In the sections of the city where the free blacks lived, there was much concern over safety. It was summer and the heat seemed to stir things up in the pot even more. Tensions were running high. When the sun went down, and darkness took over, the riots would begin all over again.

My father, Jacob Gilmore, was a greatly respected man in the community. He had helped many people in Philadelphia over the years, and now people were coming to him for advice. The colored people were afraid for their families. The abolitionists were afraid for the black people. And I, I was afraid for my father. He was all that I had left now that my mother had died.

My father assured us all, but no one was at ease during that summer of 1835 in Philadelphia.

My brother Jacob was away at university studying to be a lawyer. I always believed that he was my father's favorite. Jacob was a good man, my parents' first born, and he was black, like both of my parents. He was an honor student, kind, compassionate, and not destined to take over the family business, the bakery and confectionary which for me was my highest hope, as a woman in 1835. My father had high hopes himself for my brother Jacob to educate himself and pave a way for other black men to follow.

With my brother Jacob away at school and my mother gone, it was just me and my father left to run the bakery and the house. I wished that my brother Jacob were here now.

I'd never understood my relationship with my father, always had felt an outsider in my own home. And, it wasn't because I was the only white one in the family, it was more because I was the only person in our family who didn't know who she was. Didn't know why I was white and my family members were all black. Whenever

I asked, the only answer I ever got was that an ol' broken angel had left me on their doorstep. My mother and father had legally adopted me and I know that they truly loved me, but they adored my brother Jacob and I understood why. Still, I was jealous of my brother. Of the fact that he was the first born, of the fact that he was the same beautiful color as my mother and my father.

I would never go to university, never hold a profession, and probably never marry. I might not even ever get to run the bakery; women did not run businesses back then.

My mother had always told me, especially when I wanted to mix up a new recipe, "Some day this bakery will be all yours and you can run it however you please."

When I was fifteen she was taken by the cholera. Some people blamed the cholera on the Irish people who were coming in droves to America, living with as many as thirty people or more under the same roof. Some people called them dirty. My father just called them people, people just like us. As I always thought I might be Irish, I liked the way he put this.

Whenever anyone came into our bakery during that time of the rioting, my father made sure to wait on them himself, always sending me to the kitchen or next door to the blacksmith's on an errand. I often thought that he was embarrassed by me.

"Keep out of trouble, you hear?" my father would say. "Mind your own business, not the business of rioting."

But I could tell that even my father was a bit unnerved by the rioting, by the slave catchers, by the tension that seemed to grow more and more in the unbearable heat in the city that summer.

Sometimes Maureen and I would hide in the kitchen, stealing crumbs of sugar off from the counter, listening to the customers tell their stories. They were mostly stories of the struggles on the street. The fighting, the rioting, the hatred on the streets between the blacks and the whites. It was all so strange to me.

Still we listened, curious to know why this was all happening in our city, refusing to believe that the likes of it could ever affect us, two poor white Irish teenage girls, who'd never fully comprehended the meaning of slavery.

My father and my mother were black, but they were both free men. The thought of another human being being sold on the open market was completely incomprehensible to me.

My father's mother knew all too well, though. Her parents had been slaves in the South, both to cruel slave masters. They'd escaped his tyranny though and built themselves a new life in Philadelphia where many, many free blacks had come to build new lives. Even though I called her granny, just like my brother Jacob did, I never felt that she'd accepted me as her own grand-daughter. She never called me by my name. She never answered when I called her granny. I don't think she could believe that it was possible for her to have a white girl as a grandchild. She always called me names and worked me so hard for hours on end until finally my father would step in and say, "Enough, Ma."

All my life she'd find reasons to whip me and reasons to scold me, and reasons to point out to my parents what a terribly unappreciative child I was. But still, my mother loved me all the same and my father loved my mother and therefore seemed to love me, too. When other families children came to our bakery for treats, she always pointed out how pretty they were, how well behaved they were. She'd given them special confections that she'd baked herself from her secret recipes, and pat their heads, and send them off smiling. But she never had a kind word for me. I was not a Gilmore, she'd reminded me at least a hundred times, though she'd never told me who I really was.

She just pointed out time and again that I would never truly be accepted in the family. She didn't have to say why. I just knew. I was white, she was black. I would never and could never be her real grand-daughter.

And when my mother had died, so too had any hopes I'd had of a relationship with my grandmother. After Mama died, and Granny came in to help with the bakery on certain days, I was relegated to sweeping the floors, wiping the counters, and washing the pots and pans - though never washing them good enough. She would say, "You call this clean?" and she would wash them again herself - "The right way!" Always pointing out to my father how lazy I was.

When I was six years old, I remember one time I'd taken some polish and tried to make my skin darker, to look more like my family, my father, my mother, my brother, even my granny - maybe she'd love me then. But I was wrong - instead she'd scrubbed my skin so hard that I was red all over for a whole week.

"You are not black! Do you hear me?" Granny yelled at me. I heard her all too well. It was one of my first memories that I had of my childhood which left an indelible stain on my ego.

For this and many other reasons, I spent most of my childhood with the Irish children in the neighborhood - or I should say - with my friend Maureen Kelly and her family of thirteen siblings. Maureen Kelly, my best and my only friend for as long as I could remember. Her family was very poor. Unlike my father whose business was much respected in town, Maureen's father was a blacksmith by trade - he'd been a blacksmith in Ireland. Now he apprenticed for the blacksmith next door to our bakery, and Maureen and her whole family lived in the back room behind the blacksmith's shop. Her mother, her father, and her thirteen siblings, plus Maureen all in one room!

Maureen never complained about her situation, like I never talked about mine. People thought that we were sisters as we'd make our way through the streets of Philadelphia, sometimes people even thought us twins, we looked so much alike with our long, curly black hair, blue eyes, milky white skin with the ten freckles on either sides of our noses. We both felt like strangers - she in a new country, with an accent still strong after several years, and me as a girl born the wrong color in her family. When we were off alone in the streets of Philadelphia none of this mattered though and we made grand plans for the lives we would live when we grew older. Mary and Maury - best friends forever!

Water

"Water is a transparent, odorless, tasteless liquid."

"Never put knives with ivory handles in water. Hot water causes

them to crack and discolor."

"You're father and I have a gift for you," my mother had said, calling me to her bedside just before she'd passed away. "When you came to be with us when you were just two years old, you were wearing this."

She held out a tiny silver locket with a large "M" engraved upon it. My father tied the tiny heart-shaped locket around my neck using a beautiful black ribbon like the kind he used in his shop to tie up fancy bows for his wealthy customers.

"I'd always wanted to give you this on your sixteenth birthday," Mama said, "But I don't think that I'm going to live to see that day, Mary."

My father reached out and touched my mother's hand, and together they smiled, but seemed to be on the verge of tears. I wasn't sure if they were unshed tears of happiness or of sorrow. It was as if they and they alone shared a secret. A secret I would never be privy to.

"Wear it well," my mother said. "It's yours to keep now Miss Mary Gilmore."

I wanted to know more. My mother passed away before she could tell me though. How could my parents have purchased such an expansive give. It was probably worth more than anything on our home. She'd said that I was wearing the locket when I came to live with them. When I was two. Had someone else give me the locket with the "M" on it? But who?

~~~

For almost two years I wore that locket, always wondering what it meant. Always treasuring it because it was the last thing my mother had given me before she'd died.

"Take that thing off," my father said now as we kneaded dough together in the bakery for sweetbread. He reached up and pulled the tiny locked off from around my neck and tossed it in the trash.

I was so deeply shocked that I said nothing, but the tears drizzled down my flour covered face. I felt like I was in a dream. Why would Pa do such a wicked think to my locket? My locket that he and my mother had given to me.

He'd become terribly agitated after the last customer had left the shop that morning. It was a white man with a southern accent, asking all kinds of questions. Questions about me.

"Where's that sweet young girl I saw here yesterday in the shop?"

I was in the back, where my father made me to stay now whenever customers came in. It was all Granny's fault. Maybe Pa was beginning to believe her lies about me being lazy, or maybe it was something more. The man had left without even paying for the cakes he'd asked for. He'd said that he'd needed a receipt for some reason or other, and my father had come into the back to send me over to the blacksmith to have a receipt made out, we didn't usually give out receipts in the bakery. But when I returned through the back door with the receipt, the man had left, without getting his receipt or his cakes for that matter. I was not allowed to wear my necklace again, and was forbidden from conversing with the customers in the bakery from then on. There seemed no end to the hell that my life was becoming when the riots started up. I couldn't tell whether my father was embarrassed by me or afraid for some reason for my safety.

Father went out of his way to keep me hidden from all the visitors to our store. It seemed my Granny had gotten her wish. I was permanently relegated to the back room to clean the pots and pans, take out the garbage, and sweep the floors. This was how I was able to save my tiny locket from the trash can. I kept it hidden now under my pillow. It brought me strange dreams when I slept on it. Dreams the likes of which I'd never had before of slavery and oppression and hate.

Maria Congo never came around anymore. Though from the backroom I could often hear men talking with my father in whispered voices.

I wondered if they whispered about me. The girl with the black father in 1835 Philadelphia. We lived in dangerous times to be sure. At any given time a man or woman of color could be accused of being a runaway slave and whisked away to a strange land. I worried for my father. He clearly worried about me. It made me ill to think of what could happen to him. To us.

Then one day, Maria Congo was back. She and a stranger, a white stranger, were standing outside the window to the backroom of our shop. They seemed to be searching for something or someone. I crouched down and hid behind the long wooden table on which we rolled out our dough for the sweet breads. I didn't know why I was hiding, but I knew from somewhere deep inside that I didn't want to be seen. I could feel fear in my bones. I wanted to escape the nightmare that Philadelphia was becoming for both blacks and whites.

I thought that I had to protect my father, but maybe I was hiding to protect myself. It was so strange. I didn't even know who I was, who my real parents were. The only thing that I did know was that the only father I'd ever known was a black man, and it was no longer safe in Philadelphia for black people. The riots in the city had begun to bring great tensions now between the whites and the blacks, especially between the Irish and the blacks. Even my best friend Maury was beginning to act strangely around me.

Maury's mother was very sick now with the disease that was going around. The disease that had taken my own mother from me. Maury's mother had the cholera. Many people had died from it. Many more were very sick from it. A lot of people blamed the Irish for its rampant spread which seemed to mushroom in places where the Irish lived in close proximity.

My Granny had tried to make Maury's mother special medicines from the herbs in our garden and the honey in our cabinets, recipes she'd learned from her grandmother. Recipes that had come all the way over from Africa. But nothing seemed to work against the deadly cholera. And Maury's mother got sicker and sicker, as the chasm between us grew wider and wider.

Common Salt

"To Prevent Salt from Lumping: Mix with corn-starch, allowing one teaspoon corn-starch to six teaspoons salt. Salt is a great preservative; advantage is taken of this in salting meat and fish."

It was June and Maury and I had looked forward to spending long summer days together doing each other's hair and working on our needlepoint. With Maury's mother so sick and my father's strict rules imposed on me, it was if a dark shadow had been cast upon our well-laid plans. But we were hopeful that we might be able to get into a bit of mischief.

We'd sneak away to town on any chance we got, hoping for even the tiniest bit of adventure. But danger was in the air all over the city.

The anti-slavery and anti-abolition violence was everywhere in the city of Philadelphia, and that changed everything for us. We grew suspicious of everyone around us and of everything. Just as everyone grew suspicious of us. We even grew suspicious of one another. That was the worst part of it all.

There was a very strong anti-Irish and anti-Catholic sentiment in town that made us weary, as we were Irish, but in truth, I was a Protestant, like my family. There was a strong contention between the blacks and the Irish, as with more and more Irish coming into the shores of America, there were fewer and fewer jobs for everyone.

The slave catchers from Maryland were having a free for all in our city. And Maury and I were left to wonder what was to become of us. My parents had always taught me that the color of a person's skin on the outside did not indicate what the person was like on the inside. Like an onion, there were many layers to each and every person. But in the city of brotherly love in 1835, there did not seem to be much love going around, only hate.

When I'd told Maury how strange my father had been acting and how he'd made me take off my necklace, she shook her head and said something was awry.

"Why do you think that your father made you take it off?" Maury had asked me. "Some people in town are saying that there are slave catchers here from Maryland looking for a white slave girl. Maybe it's you!"

I laughed. Maury could be such a jerk sometimes. "Maybe it's you!" I'd said.

She'd stared at me very solemnly and said, "My father is not black, Mary."

I'd had enough. I thought she was crazy and I stared her down, in essence telling her that she was acting like an idiot, or an "eejit" as she would have said with her Irish brogue, without having to say a single word. My father was not a slave and never had been

"My eyes are as blue as yours," I told her.

"Some slaves have blue eyes," she'd replied.

"My skin is *whiter* than yours," I'd said.

To this Maury said nothing. She knew that she could never get the better of me, though she often tried.

"You're right," she said, trying to shrug our conversation off, "I was only kidding with you. Geez, you get so upset sometimes."

But she'd opened up thoughts in my mind that I'd never even dared to consider before. There were things about myself that I might never come to know, might never want to know.

My past was a secret. A story never told to me by my mother or my father. And now the only puzzle piece I had from my past, my tiny locket with the "M" engraved upon it, was being taken away from me. Surprisingly, I suddenly cared not a bit for the locket and the secrets it held. I was Mary Gilmore, a white Irish girl with a black father who was a free man. Whoever the slave catcher was looking for, whatever her complexion might be, it was not me. Of this I was sure.

I wanted to believe this, but as we walked through the streets of the city that night back to my father's bakery amidst the placards warning fugitive slaves to be alert for the slave catchers who were freely roaming the city now, I understood that no one, no one was safe now in the city of brotherly love. No one was safe from the slave catcher's ugly snare, not even white Irish girls like me.

Milk

"Why milk sours. A germ found floating in the air attacks a
portion of the lactose."

All that week, whenever I was finished with my work in the bakery and Maury was finished taking care of her mother and her thirteen brothers and sisters, which was not often, we'd run out to the field to play. Though we were no longer children, in fact we were far from it, we were seventeen, almost eighteen, and foolishly believed that we were far removed from the troubles. We both planned to marry soon and have families of our own, even though neither of us and any potential suitors. Still that did not keep us from dreaming.

It was a lazy, very hazy summer evening in downtown Philadelphia and Maury and I had made our way out to the furthest side of the field where the boys were playing ball. We were giddy and laughing and trying to get their attention.

As often was the case with Maury and I, we were planning our futures, pointing out possible suitors on the playing field. We both liked Samuel Allen, the Irish immigrant who'd come over to America when we were eight.

We were making fools of ourselves to be sure, because the boys were now starting to stare at us, but we didn't care. We liked it a little. Who doesn't like it when a cute boy takes notice of you, we laughed, then laughed some more, a little louder, until Samuel finally took notice and came across the field to sit with us.

He looked so handsome, even though he was covered in dirt from playing in the muddy field with all the other boys. His eyes were a deep blue like mine. His hair was dark and curly. And his skin, which was usually so milky white was red with sunburn.

"Good evening ladies," he said in a sing-song way with a strong Irish brogue. "Nice night for a walk."

Maury and I giggled like two school girls, nodding politely.

Samuel leaned in and touched his finger to the locket around my neck.

"Lovely necklace, Mary," he said.

I felt a flush of heat at his touch. I knew I shouldn't have worn the necklace, should have kept it hidden in its secret hiding place beneath my pillow. But it was so lovely and we were going to the fields and it made me feel special. Still no excuse could be made for my wearing it that would suffice. My father had explicitly told me not to wear it, but I had. As soon as Samuel took notice of if, I felt guilty, uneasy, as though I'd made a terrible mistake. I wanted to run all the way home.

He saw how uncomfortable I'd suddenly become. "What are you two up to?" he asked with a lilt in his voice.

Everyone always thought that of Maury and me. That was were up to something. Always thought that we were up to no good, racing around the streets of Philadelphia, getting into mischief, not bad mischief, just teenage girl mischief.

Maury glanced sideways at me winking in my direction, intimating that what were doing was for us to know and for Samuel Allen to find out. We made a game out of everything. That was really just it, for Maury and me, all our life had been a game, but now that we were seventeen and becoming adults, it was becoming a dangerous game.

Samuel just laughed at us and ran back onto the field with the other boys. "Have it your way," he'd called over his shoulder to us.

And we did. We always did. Maury and I always did have it our way.

As Samuel ran off he looked back at me, just a quick glance, but I swore he stared straight into my soul.

"Did you see the way he looked at me?" Maury asked.

I just laughed. "He looked straight at me," I said. That was the problem with Maury and me, we looked exactly alike, but we say things very differently. Samuel was clearly looking at me.

My mother and father had been seventeen when they had met. I was almost eighteen. It was not hard for me to imagine having Samuel Allen as a husband. Having Samuel Allen as the father of my children. Mrs. Samuel Allen. Mrs. Mary Gilmore Allen. Yes, I liked the sound of it.

"You shouldn't make plans that you can't keep," Maury said, interrupting my train of thoughts about my future with Samuel. Her voice sounded very harsh. All the laughter of a moment ago had evaporated into the heat of the evening. "You shouldn't lead him on, because he is going to be a doctor someday, and his family would never, never allow him to marry you, Mary."

I could see Samuel standing with the other boys in the field. He was still staring at me, and all I could see was his blue eyes through the amazing pink dusk of the evening.

"Stop staring at him, Mary!" Maury demanded now.

"I'm not staring at him!" I said, but I knew I was lying to my friend and to myself. I wondered what other lies I'd told myself and believed. I feared that there may be a great many things that were just bubbling up under the surface from my past.

When my brother Jacob came home unexpectedly from the university, I was excited to see him, but frightened as well. It was so unlike him to leave his studies. He must have had a very good reason to return without a words notice. All of the neighbors came by to see my big brother, returned from university. But I could only wonder, why?

Jacob was no longer a boy now. He was a man, and a smart looking man as well. A refined black gentleman attending university. My father's eyes beamed with pride. His son, the college man. Jacob was the only person in our family ever to attend university. In fact he was the only person on our whole street attending university. He carried a tremendous responsibility, the weight of the dreams of all his friends and family, all of his ancestors, upon his broad shoulders. He had to do well, for all of us - so why had he returned now?

"I missed you, that's why," he told me, giving me a big hug. I'd missed him too, ever since he'd left for school, nothing had been the same in our house or our town.

"You're a woman now," Jacob said.

"Almost," I said, "I will turn eighteen in two months time."

"Well, that's something to celebrate!" he said, and celebrate we did. That night we had a special dinner and invited all of our friends and neighbors. My father clearly wanted to show off his son, the college man, just returned from over a year's absence.

Father wore his Sunday clothes and Granny made some of her favorite secret recipes. Everyone was in great spirits and listened eagerly to all of my brother's stories of what college was like, though everyone in the room knew that none of us would ever get there to see it with our own eyes. We were all happy for Jacob. He was a good student getting all A's and hoping to go on to law school so that he could practice in the field of law and help with the abolitionist movement to free all the slaves in the United States. He hoped to come back and settle in Philadelphia and set up his practice there some day. Philadelphia he said was the heart of the abolition movement. Philadelphia, Boston, and New York all had strong anti-slavery societies, he said. He knew that in his lifetime he would see an end to slavery. His words gave us all hope.

I watched as my brother Jacob spoke of his grand plans and prayed that he was correct. Prayed that I, too, would see an end to slavery in my lifetime. Even though he was my brother, it felt like a special privilege to have Jacob in our home again. Everyone listened as he told of what was going on in the anti-slavery societies throughout the North. Almost all of our guests were black, except for Maury's family, and they all eagerly listened as Jacob told of the abolitionists, the anti-slavery societies, and the great many speeches against slavery that were going on everywhere now.

"Let's go to one!" I said to my father in the hopes of hearing a speech like the ones of which Jacob was speaking. Jacob immediately stopped talking and my father grew suddenly stone faced for the first time that evening. All the excited chattering came to a complete and sudden stop. Everyone was staring at me.

What had I said that was wrong?

Since I had taken over Jacob's old room when he'd gone away to school, it seemed only right now to give him back his room when he returned. I moved my few things back into the small room I'd used to use. I was happy to do this for my brother. Happy he was home and we were all a family again. I wished our mother could be there with us. She'd be so proud of the man that Jacob was becoming.

My brother had brought a great many newspaper clippings with him that he had collected while he was away at college. They all dealt with the anti-slavery movement. There were horrible stories of fugitive slaves who had been captured in the North by slave catchers, some who had been free men for as much as 23 years, who had opened businesses and had families and were captured and put back into bondage after decades of freedom. There were advertisements for the sale of slaves, slaves sold like cattle on the open market. There were advertisements too for runaway slaves. There were copies of great speeches made by famous orators against slavery, and warnings to free black men to beware of slave catchers in the North. I wondered when he found the time to study if he read so many newspapers.

A few days after my brother had come home, many men I didn't recognize came to the bakery to speak with my father and my brother. My Granny sent me off to play with Maury.

Maury's mother had become even more seriously ill with the cholera and Maury seemed set on venting her anger in my direction. She seemed more jealous of me now than ever before, and even more jealous of my brother Jacob and all the attention he was getting from everyone in the neighborhood.

"You must be upset now that your brother is home and you don't have your own room anymore," Maury said.

"I'm happy Jacob's home," I said, surprised Maury could think so little of me.

"But you have to sleep in that storage closet again," Maury said, "You can't seriously be happy about that!"

I suddenly wanted to say something mean and vindictive to Maury. I wanted to say my small storage closet beat the small room that the fifteen people in her family all slept in by a long shot -- but I didn't. My father had always taught me that if you don't have anything nice to say, it was better to say nothing at all. Still it was difficult to hold my tongue.

"Oh no!" I cried changing the subject, "There are so many more of those fugitive slave placards posted." I pointed to a row of them along a wall through the center of town.

"Let's go see what they say," Maury said, racing off ahead of me in their direction.

"Are you crazy?" I said. "I don't want to read that stuff."

"Suit yourself," Maury said and plucked one off, folding it neatly and placing it in her pocket. As we walked home to Maury's house, I wanted to ask her if I could read it, but changed my mind. I really didn't want to know what any slave catcher had written.

Maury was making cabbage soup for dinner, and asked me if I wanted to stay. She knew all too well, that whenever I was invited to dinner at her house, I always brought with me something special and delicious from my father's bakery, usually a nice loaf of bread or a cake fresh baked that morning. Maury had really made me mad though, first with her comment about my brother and then with her interest in the slave catcher's posters.

"Not tonight," I said. Maury was changing, and I was not sure I liked the direction she was moving in.

Maybe Maury was right. Just a little bit, about how I felt about my brother Jacob. I wasn't angry he was home, not at all, but maybe in truth I was just the tiniest bit envious of Jacob and of the life he was destined to lead.

Jacob was going to be a lawyer. He was going to help our people rise up from slavery and all become free men at last. When I thought this to myself, I paused, "Our people." I'd used the word "our" as if somehow I finally belonged in my family, no longer the white outcast. I smiled at this feeling of belonging which I was experiencing for perhaps the first time. "Our people."

"You're smile is lovely," my brother said, "What are you thinking about, Mary?"

"I was thinking about you, my favorite brother, whose going to become a lawyer someday and make a difference in this world."

"You have high hopes for me," he said.

"We all do, Jacob."

Jacob was the kindest man I ever knew. He was just like our father, but more open with his feelings.

"How did I get so lucky to have you for a sister?" he said as we began to clear the dinner dishes from the table.

"That is one question I'd love the answer to," I said smiling back at him.

Jacob knew full well what I was asking. He was surely privy to my background. He knew how it had come to pass that I had come to be Jacob Gilmore's daughter. I was sure of it. But he was loyal to my father and our family and always would be.

He simply smiled and said, "I sure do have a debt of gratitude to that ol' broken angel who left you on our doorstep."

I wondered if I would ever to come to know the truth, ever come to know how a poor white Irish girl like me came to be left on Jacob Gilmore's doorstep. Little did I know that day was soon at hand.

I saw Samuel Allen that next day. He'd come to the bakery for bread for his mother, though I wanted to think that he came to see me. But that didn't happen.

My father still held fast to his rule that I work only in the back room. So I couldn't see Samuel and he couldn't see me, but through the open door to the backroom. He tried to get my attention, but it would not have been proper for me to acknowledge his advances, especially under my father's watchful eye.

I sat on the stool in the back room, pretending to busy myself at something or other, as my father waited on Samuel himself. Maybe he'll ask about me, maybe ask to court me even, I blushed at the thought of Samuel Allen asking my father if he could court me.

Then, quite unexpectedly, Samuel walked over to the counter and waved right in my direction, right in front of my father!

"Beautiful day out there, Miss Mary! Nice night for a walk. Maybe I'll see you and Maury later in the park?"

I thought that I would faint! He hadn't just said that in front of my father, had he? But he had, and for some reason, I was glad for it. He wanted to meet me in the park tonight.

"It is indeed, Master Samuel. Perhaps we shall see you later."

I knew that it was not prudent for me to be so forthright in my father's presence and I knew that Samuel Allen had come calling for me. I knew he hadn't really come in just for a loaf of bread.

I'm not sure whether my father was happy for me or not about Samuel's visit. If he was, he certainly didn't say anything about it.

And if he weren't, he hadn't forbidden me from going to the park that evening with Maury. I just remember the overwhelming silence of that moment when for the first time in my life my father saw me as a woman and not a little girl. I knew I was growing up in that instant. But had not the slightest idea of where I was headed. Perhaps to the alter with Samuel Allen!

Maury had agreed reluctantly to go to the park that evening with me, though she feigned all kinds of excuses to get out of going. She just didn't want for me to end up with Samuel Allen, I was sure of that. Her envy was turning her blue eyes green in color.

I had convinced her to go by bribing her with spice cookies, many, many spice cookies, of which I'm sure my father would have been angry about, had he noticed them missing. I'd stolen the cookies from my father in the name of love. Surely, I would be punished by my father or by fate for my crime. But it didn't seem to matter, just so long as I could see Samuel.

Little did I know that fate would respond so quickly to my treachery.

Second Course: Black and White and Read All Over

"Tie strands of a new broom closely together, put into a pail of boiling water, and soak two hours. Dry thoroughly before using. Before sweeping old carpets, sprinkle with pieces of newspaper wrung out of water. After sweeping, wipe over with a cloth wrung out of a weak solution of ammonia water, which seems to brighten colors."

-- The Boston Cooking School Cook Book by Fannie Merritt Farmer

Paper

"Turn grate back into place, remove the covers over fire-box, and cover grate with pieces of paper (twisted in centre and left loose at the ends). Cover paper with small sticks, or pieces of pine wood, being sure that the wood reaches the ends of fire-box, and so arranged that it will admit air."

It was a lovely summer evening, filled with laughter from the children who ran free in the park and twinkles from the fire-flies were just beginning to appear in the clover. I could see Samuel across the field with a few other of the Irish boys from the neighborhood. My heart was beating as fast as the drums at the parades on Independence Day.

Surely, nothing could be as wonderful as this feeling that had crept into my soul. Was it love? Perhaps I was just imagining it, but Samuel seemed to feel the same way I did. Maury on the other hand was look a bit green as she swallowed the last crumb of the fourth spice cookie that I'd given her.

Samuel had barely had time to say hello, when Maury pulled the newspaper clipping out from her skirt pocket.

"Did you see what was in the paper today?" she said almost giddy with enthusiasm over the news she held in her hand which trembled with excitement.

Before either Samuel or I could respond, Maury began to read the clipping aloud to us. E.D. Ingraham, the slave trader from Maryland had published a letter in the newspaper stating that he was searching for information on a free mother, Milly Winder, in Philadelphia, who had given birth to a daughter, Emily, while in bondage. The slave holder, Robert Aitkins of Baltimore, wanted Emily back, as she was his property. The mother, Milly, had been emancipated, but the daughter had not. The child had disappeared more than ten years before and all traces of her existence were now gone. Milly Winder had been a mulatto and the baby's father was white. The child Emily would be about seventeen now and would probably attempt to pass for a white person. Any person who would harbor or conceal the fugitive Emily Winder would be fined or imprisoned or both. Mr. Aitkins, the slave holder, wished to retrieve the fugitive Emily in all haste. It was rumored as of late that the girl was living in Philadelphia. "She is said to be the finest looking woman in this country." Any information should be delivered to William Swift or E.D. Ingraham, both acting as counsel and agent for the demandant, Robert Aitkins. Reward offered.

Maury smiled a sinister smile when she told us about the excitement the story from the paper had caused in town.

"A mulatto slave secretly passing herself off as a white person in Philadelphia, can you imagine?" Maury said with a hint of sarcasm in her voice.

"Do you know something that we don't, Maureen?" Samuel asked.

I on the other hand had been rendered speechless, my knees began to buckle beneath me and the air had constricted in my lungs.

I wanted to scream, "Shut up! Shut up! Shut up!" But I was too terrified to even whisper. I thought of the 'M' engraved on my necklace. Could it possibly have stood for Milly?

Did I now know what I'd always wanted to know? The thing was, I found that I no longer wanted to know.

Blood trickled out of the corner of my brow and into my eyes, making it difficult for me to make out just who it was that was standing over me.

Samuel and Maury were propping my head up. I didn't know what had happened. But I was sick to my stomach, and had a violent headache. I didn't know how it was that I'd come to be lying on the ground in the park, until Samuel told me.

"You fainted," he said, "Are you alright?"

"I don't think so," Maury said. "We'd better take her home."

They brought me back to my yard and we all sat on the stoop outside the bakery storefront. Horrible thoughts of bondage filled my mind. I couldn't escape the reality of what Maury had implied as she'd read from that newspaper clipping. It couldn't be true!

Maury was too preoccupied flirting with Samuel to take any notice of the pain she'd inflicted upon me. She clearly thought this was all just a game, just a mischievous game, the likes of which we'd played a thousand times before, but with giggles, and laughter, not treachery like this. She couldn't possibly understand what she was implying. Or could she? Could she have that much hate in her heart?

Samuel walked Maury back to her house and I was glad to be rid of her. I saw that my father was reading the newspaper at the long wooden table upon which we kneaded so many loaves of bread together. There were tears in his eyes, and I knew then that this was not just another of Maury's fabrications. My father's eyes contained something I'd never seen in them before -- fear.

I tossed the remaining spice cookie crumbs that I'd stolen earlier onto the grass for the birds. I'd surely brought this trouble all upon myself with my mischief. My father was a good man. How could I bring him so much pain when all he'd ever given me was happiness.

It seemed as if every single person in Philadelphia was whispering about the story in the newspapers. Rumors about Milly and Maria Congo and my father and I were rampant. The talk on the street was that I was Emily that the story spoke of.

My father vehemently denied it.

Most people stood with my father, on his side, absolutely positive that I could not possibly be the Emily spoken of in the story in the newspapers. Others insisted that it had to be true, why else would a black man take in and adopt a white child. It just wasn't done. It certainly seemed more logical to them that I was a black fugitive slave simply pretending to be white.

Maria Congo had turned me into E.D. Ingraham, the slave holder's agent as being the Emily he was looking for, and not it was only a matter of time before I would be arrested.

Maria Congo, the old black woman who'd stolen food and money from my father's bakery for years without ever being turned over to the authorities by my father, had turned me over for the reward money, turned me in as a fugitive slave, a runaway. Could her lies possibly be true?

Everyone knew how difficult it was for a person accused of being a fugitive slave to be found innocent of the charge. So many free blacks had been wrongfully accused, arrested, and found guilty. Ultimately, being turned over to the slaveholders. Proving one's innocence on accusations of being a runaway slave was virtually impossible. Witnesses and birth records or papers were required. I had no such documents, unless the old broken angel that my parents had always told me about somehow miraculously appeared now. Of course, this was highly unlikely, as at seventeen, I was too old to believe in angels coming down from heaven to save me, still, I wanted to believe. I wanted to believe my father, as he assured me again and again it was all lies. I was not Emily. I was Mary, Mary Gilmore.

I wanted to believe that Maury, my best friend, had not meant to be vindictive and mean when she read the story to Samuel and me. I wanted to believe that this nightmare would end when I awoke the next morning and things would all go back to normal and I could again think of things like Samuel Allen and raising a family of my own, and not about things like whether I was a runaway slave who was about to be put into bondage. I wanted to believe I was a white Irish girl living in a wonderful black family. I wanted to believe that everything would go back to the way it had been.

But it could not. Nothing would ever be the same again.

The next morning they came for me, to arrest me. I didn't want to be seen, I hid behind the long wooden table in the bakery, as my father had told me to do for the past few weeks. Why hadn't I listened then? I peeked over the table and could make out the men who would be my captors. This couldn't be happening to me. I was white!

So I ran. I ran out the back door of my house. I ran across the back yard. I ran down South Sixth Street. I ran up Spruce. I could hear people screaming at me to stop.

"Stop! Stop!" the voices cried.

But I could not stop. I could not let them catch me to arrest me as a runaway slave. The idea was crazy -- or was it? I myself couldn't answer that question. There was a part of me then that remembered something from my past. All I could think now as I ran breathless through the streets of Philadelphia was what it would be like to be in bondage. To be whipped. To be owned. To be another man's property. To be treated like cattle or worse.

So I ran. I ran until my legs could run no more and the screams descended upon me. There were six or seven large men and they grabbed me roughly and lifted me up off from the ground.

I assured them it was a mistake. I was not a fugitive slave. But they would not listen to me. I saw as my father struggled to help me, but he was no match for the many men who held me face down in the street and bound me up. They put large bracelets around my wrists, but not bracelets made of gold or of silver. I was put into shackles made of iron and steel connected by heavy chains. I was dragged most violently to the court house, being called nigger all the way by these wicked men.

Sometimes you wait all your life for a dream to come true, and when it does, you realize you'd been dreaming the wrong dream. All my life I had wanted to be black like my parents, like my brother, like my family. All my life I'd wanted to know who I really was and why I was white. The ugly duckling in a family of swans.

My dream had turned into a nightmare. All I could hope for now was to wake up. I prayed that my father had been telling me the truth all those years. I prayed for my ol' broken angel to fly down to earth and save me now when I needed her the most.

I would never wish upon anyone, man or beast, the evils of slavery. As I sat in my cell at the jail, badly beaten and bruised, I promised to never doubt my father's love again. It was June 13, 1835, a day I shall never, never be able to erase from my memory. I prayed that God would not judge me too severely for the mischief I'd caused in my youth, for my stealing of cookies and sweets from father's store, of my lying and wearing my locket.

"I've done terrible things," I said out loud, alone in my jail cell, "I deserve this I guess."

"No you don't," the angel on the other side of the prison bars said, it was my father. The Honorable Judge Randall had set my bail at $1,000.00 when I was arrested. $1,000.00! Nobody had that kind of money that I knew.

The magistrate had taken the oath of the demandant, Robert Aitkins, the slave holder, the man who claimed that I was his property. In my heart of hearts I knew that I'd never laid eyes upon this man in my life. Not ever before. Still, there was this white gentleman, under oath, saying that I was his slave, Emily Winder.

"Why do you think it's me? How could you think it's me? I'm not Emily!" I wanted to scream, but kept silent and still in my iron shackles and chains in the jail cell.

Then my father had come, Jacob Gilmore, the real angel in my story. I could only imagine how his heart must have been breaking to see me shackled and chained, accused of being a fugitive slave, bonnetless and sooty, destined for a life of servitude now as a slave to a lying and cruel slave master.

As soon as I saw my father I began to cry.

I took off the tiny locket with the 'M' on it and passed it silently through the iron bars to my father.

"I'm sorry," I said.

"Don't be. You ain't done nothing to be sorry for. Do you hear me. You ain't Emily Winder. You are Mary Gilmore. My daughter. Do you hear me? You're my daughter, and ain't no slave holder gonna get his hands on you. Not in my lifetime!"

I had never noticed how fiercely proud my father was. Fiercely proud -- of me! I suddenly believed everything was going to be alright.

"But the bail, pa. The bail has been set at $1,000.00!" I said.

And just like that, I was free on bail. I hadn't but said $1,000.00, and the jailor was opening the door to my cell and unshackling my bloodied wrists and ankles. I didn't know what exactly was happening, but I didn't care at that moment. I was free and I flung myself wildly into the open arms of my father, Jacob Gilmore, my hero, my angel.

"But how, Pa?" I asked, very much confused by everything that had transpired on that day.

"One thousand dollars, child, that ain't nothing. I guess you never knew that your old man was a wealthy old black man, now did you?"

I had no idea what my father was talking about. Where could he possibly have come up with that much money.

"Mary, you surely didn't think that your father was a fool. Jacob's in college, you wear pretty dresses and read and write so well, taking all your piano lessons, and such. Did you ever stop to think where all that money came from?"

"I certainly had not. I guess I'd taken it all for granted. All of it. No wonder Maury was jealous of me. Her family was so poor. I felt badly now for the hurt feelings between us.

"The judge accepted me as your surety. I put down the $1,000.00 for your bail, though I would have put down $10,000.00 if that's what it would have taken. You're my child. My child. And no one can't never prove otherwise."

"But," I said.

"But nothing," he interrupted. "I legally adopted you. I raised you. I schooled you. I loved you as my own. You are not black and you are not a fugitive slave. Just try and let anyone prove otherwise. Just try. You are my Mary. Mary Gilmore. Do you hear me?"

"Yes, Pa." I felt so safe as he held my hand which still bled a tiny bit from the shackles and we walked side by side out of the jail house. I felt so proud to bear his name. To be his daughter. Mary Gilmore, Jacob Gilmore's white daughter.

People filled the streets outside the jail house.

They cheered as my father and I made our way to our carriage. I felt a sense of new found pride in my father, in myself, and in this the city of brother love, that stood behind my father and I on this the worst day of my life. If I live to be one hundred years old, I will never forget that moment, that feeling, we were going to fight that slave owner, Robert Aitkins. We were going to fight him and we were going to win!

I never realized just how evil men could be. I never realized how kind they could be also.

All that next day neighbors, both black and white flooded our bakery with warm wishes.

My brother Jacob came home and brought with him newspaper clippings from all over about my case.

I wanted to know how this could be happening to us and I needed to know why. I knew if anyone could answer my questions it was my brother Jacob.

I understood now fully why he wanted to study the law and protect our people, all people from wrongs such as was happening to me. I didn't know how I was going to get out of this mess I was in, but with my father and my brother by my side, I felt certain anything was possible.

I asked Jacob to help me understand what was happening to me and he tried to explain in terms that I would understand. The Pennsylvania Abolition society was providing my legal assistance, still I wanted to hear it straight from my brother Jacob.

Jacob told me that any white man could claim another man, woman, or child was his alleged slave. All a man needed to prove that another was his property was to go before a justice of the peace with an affidavit asserting his claim, even if the affidavit was completely bogus.

He told me that we were lucky that we lived in the city of Philadelphia, because there were only three states in the country in which a person who was claimed to be an alleged slave was entitled to a trial by a jury of one's peers. In some states Jacob told me it was easier to claim another person as one's slave than it was to recover a stolen pig from one's neighbor.

Jacob was not making me to feel very reassured, but I implored him to continue, as my trial was set to begin on the morrow, June 14th at 1 o'clock.

Ink

"To Remove An Ink Stain: From linens, piques, lawns, madras, batistes, percales, cheviots, ginghams, organdies, and all other wash fabrics, don't wear them out by destructive rubbing with soap and wash-board. Pearline does more than soap can do -- without rubbing. That's why the most delicate wash fabrics last twice as long when Pearline does the washing."

Legalized kidnapping is what Jacob called it. Some people called it "the reverse Underground Railroad." And I'd been kidnapped all right. There were more riots now in the streets as the tensions rose higher. Anti-abolitionists turned against abolitionists. Blacks against whites. Protestants against Catholics. The people were fighting over their rights under the Constitution. Rights to freedom. Rights to property. Rights to religion. Rights I no longer had as an alleged runaway slave.

If found guilty of being a fugitive slave, I became another man's property. I went from being white to black. If found guilty I would know that God had failed me, found me unworthy, my ol' broken angel had given up on me, and I would lose my religion, too. If found guilty, I would lose my name, my race, my religion, my family and my freedom.

Samuel had come over to see if I was alright. He'd heard about what had happened and was concerned about me.

"Everything is going to be alright," he said.

I prayed he was right.

I knew like everyone else knew in Philadelphia that anything could happen. I knew in my heart that I was Mary Gilmore, but others believed me to be Emily Winder, fugitive slave.

"I know that you're Mary Gilmore," Samuel said. "And someday, I hope you'll be Mary Gilmore Allen."

And suddenly, there was a purpose to my vindication, to my proving myself without question to being Mary Gilmore, daughter of Jacob Gilmore, the baker and not Emily Winder the fugitive slave. I had to win in court tomorrow, so that I could become Mary Gilmore Allen, wife of Samuel Allen.

"I hope so, too," I said. My eyes were burning as I fought back tears that pounded at my eyelids. "I hope so, too."

That was when I made the promise to myself to defeat the monster who was attempting to kidnap me -- kidnap me legally!

I needed to understand better the law and how it worked before I stepped into the courtroom the next day. It was going to take all the courage I could muster to walk into that court room as an alleged runaway slave, an alleged felon, and to walk out a free woman, triumphant. I went to talk with my brother Jacob some more about what to expect, what to do. Though I knew that there was very little that I could do.

Jacob was in the back room at the long table with my father who was kneading bread, it was a place of strange comfort for us. It reminded us of our mother. It was where we where a family. My father was silent as he pounded out his frustrations on the dough.

"Could you answer a few more questions for me?" I asked.

"What did you have in mind?" Jacob said.

"How much trouble am I really in?"

My father looked up for just a moment from the dough he was pounding mercilessly into the table.

"Are you sure that you really want to know?" was all Jacob said.

"I do," I said with great trepidation.

My father took such a violent swing at the dough that his fist came down with a thunderous Whomp! On the table top. I could see he was terrified for me, for us, for our family. Still, I needed to know the truth, no matter how badly he wanted to protect me. Would I be home again tomorrow evening after the trial, or would I be headed for Maryland in bondage?

"Where should I begin," Jacob asked himself.

First he told me about a book by Judge Stroud of Philadelphia that had been written recently. According to this Judge Stroud, more than thirty free black persons had been kidnapped recently in Philadelphia in just a two year period, and most of them had been children.

My father looked up at Jacob now with such anger in his eyes, I truly thought that he was going to slap Jacob across the face with his flour covered hand.

"What?" Jacob said defensively to my father. "You know it's true. Would you rather I lied to her? Sugar-coated her situation and said it was all going to be alright."

"Continue," my father said solemnly.

I wasn't sure that I wanted to hear any more, but Jacob went on.

"It didn't make a bit of difference what the color of you skin is. Slaves can be as dark as charcoal or as white as sugar, your complexion don't make a bit of difference. If a slave catcher comes calling with a warrant, men, women, and children with snow white skin, blue eyes, and blond hair are continuously sold at the slave auctions, but not so many as the blacks. They have it a lot harder."

I think he saw that I was on the verge of tears, because he then relayed to me how much infinitely easier it was for a person of my fair complexion to prove my innocence than it was for a person of color.

When I had been younger, I remember hearing the stories of the runaways, of the fugitives. I remember the interest my brother and my father had taken in ever single case. How my father had gone out of his way to assist every one of them that happened in our jurisdiction.

I had been more interested in my dolls and playing silly games with Maury next door.

I felt so ashamed now for my apathy all of the years. Naively assuming it could never happen to me, I hadn't tried to do anything to make it easier for those that it had been happening to.

It was late in the evening, my father and my brother were long gone off to bed, still I tossed and turned, unable to sleep for the thought of the impending trial set to begin tomorrow.

Perhaps I was asleep and this had all been a bad dream. It felt like a bad dream. Even the papers that Jacob had brought asserted as much.

Of "The Case of Mary Gilmore" as all the newspapers were calling it, the Pennsylvania Courier wrote, "This is the singular and it is believed the unprecedented circumstance, of the complexion of the respondent being to all appearances entirely white."

The Inquirer said that notion was absurd and cited my father, Jacob Gilmore, "a man of exemplary life and unimpeachable integrity."

The Liberator Newspaper read, "Mary Gilmore, a young girl of this name with a white skin and entirely devoid of any indication of African extraction was recently claimed as a slave, apprehended, and taken before Judge Randall of Philadelphia." This report ominously read, "To be continued." I couldn't wait to read how it all turned out.

Poulson's Advertiser was very flattering, "The trial of Mary Gilmore, the young and interesting female whose case has excited so much public sympathy in Philadelphia" is set to begin tomorrow. I'd never considered myself interesting, but there it was in print.

Many papers cited my situation as "legalized kidnapping" just as my brother had said. And a newspaper called The Emporium read, "A laudable indignation was universally manifested among our citizens on Saturday last by the exposure of a woman apprehended and put on trial as an alleged slave in Philadelphia. The young woman is as white as any of your citizens; indeed we scarcely ever saw a child with a fairer or clearer complexion than this lass."

I pinned each newspaper clipping up on my wall, stunned by my instant celebrity in the papers. A celebrity the likes of which no one could be envious however, especially after reading the clipping from The Register.

"Dealing in slaves," it read, "has become a large business; establishments are made in several places in Maryland and Virginia at which they are sold like cattle. These places of deposit are strongly built, and well supplied with iron thumb screws and gags, and ornamented with cow skins and other whips, often times bloody."

Mr. Aitkins, the slave holder who makes the claims against me is from Baltimore. I shuddered to think of the horrors of what could happen to me in Maryland if I were to lose in court the next day.

Had anyone ever told me in days past that this was what my future held for me, I would have laughed at them. I had never heard of white slaves, even though I'd lived all my life with people who knew a great deal about slavery and were staunch abolitionists. No wonder my Granny had though me unappreciative for all that my father had done for me over the years. She was right, I had been ungrateful. I hadn't understood what it meant for them to be free and black in a dangerous time such as this.

I was white, how could I have known. I was a child, a silly white Irish child who didn't understand how very far out of their way my parents had gone to protect me. No I did and I made a solemn vow just before the sun rose on the day of my trial. If I were to be set free, to be found innocent, to be allowed to remain Mary Gilmore, I would spend the rest of my days in the service of others, protecting their rights, and the rights of all men to be free.

Third Course: A Baker's Dozen

"Ways of Keeping Eggs.

I. Pack in sawdust, small end down.

II. Keep in lime water.

III. From July to September a large number of eggs are packed, small ends down, in cases having compartments, one for each egg and kept in cold storage. Eggs are often kept in cold storage six months, and then sold as cooking eggs"

    -- The Boston Cooking School Cook Book by Fannie Merritt Farmer

Planked Eggs

"Finely chop cold cooked corned beef or corned tongue; there should be two-thirds cup. Add an equal quantity of fine bread crumbs, moisten with cream and season with salt and pepper. Spread mixture on plank, and make nests and border of duchess potatoes, using rose tube. Put a buttered or poached egg in each nest and put in oven to brown potato. Garnish with tomatoes cut in halves and broiled and parsley. Eggs may be sprinkled buttered cracker crumbs, *just before sending to oven*, if preferred."

The next morning when I woke up, the streets were alive with rioting. I didn't remember falling asleep, but I knew I must have, because somewhere between the still of the night when I tossed in my bed afraid for the dawn to come and now, several hundred people had gathered outside of my home on South Sixth Street and were wreaking havoc clear up past Eighth Street near the court house. I could hear my father shuffling about down in the kitchen, a nervous ball of energy.

My knees felt weak beneath me. Too weak in fact to hold me up. I wished I could go back to bed and never ever have to leave the safety of my home again.

It appeared that not only myself and my father were restless, in deed, the whole of Philadelphia seemed restless in anticipation of my trial which was scheduled to being at one o'clock sharp before the Honorable Judge Randall. Twelve jurors and one alternate had been selected for my jury, a jury of peers. It was obvious that no one knew exactly how to interpret the meaning of peer in my case, the case of Mary Gilmore, as it was now being called. Half the jury was made up of free black men and the other half was made up of white men. The alternate was white as well.

I saw them eye me with curiosity as they entered the court room trying to solve the mystery for themselves. Was she black or was she white? I could hear their thoughts as the entered the jury box. I didn't like the way that they were looking at me. I felt like a spectacle. I was a spectacle. The curiosity of Philadelphia. The white girl accused of being a runaway slave, in jeopardy of losing her freedom for ever if she couldn't prove the color of her skin to be white.

I didn't feel very well at all.

The look on my father's face as the judge entered was solemn. He was sitting with my brother Jacob and Samuel Allen and it seemed everyone else in the neighborhood. There were newspaper reporters there and even Maury Kelly had come with her father.

People had come out of the woodwork for my trial. They spilled out into the streets and down the side alleys.

Judge Randall made it very clear from the outset that he wouldn't stand for any hullabaloo or revelry in his courtroom. Which made me feel a bit better, as the sheer magnitude of the crowd had made me fall a queasiness like a motion sickness from the flood of people.

After he'd laid out the fact of my case and the preliminaries for the jury, my trial got underway.

In essence, as a runaway slave, I was being accused of stealing myself from my master, which was a felony under federal law. I thought to myself of the cookies I had stolen from my father for Maury and the cookies and sweetbreads Maria Congo had stolen from my father. She was there, Maria Congo. She narrowed her eyes at me in the court room as if to say, I got you back now. Maria Congo, witness for the claimant Robert Aitkins. I couldn't believe such maliciousness could exist in someone's heart. Someone we'd been so kind to all those years.

I loathed the sight of her in that court room. Loathed the glaring stare she gave my father. The trial was taking a toll on him. I could see that as he held his chest and hung his head. The trial had only just begun and already it had aged my father by ten years or more.

It took a very long time in the way of opening remarks and introductions. A guard stood by the back door, I assumed to catch me if I tried to escape.

Finally, the trial got underway at half past one in the afternoon. The counsel for the defendant, Mr. Aitkins agent Mr. William Swift was sworn in as a witness. He was a mean and a hard looking man, hard and unyielding in his demeanor on the stand.

Mr. Swift testified that Robert Aitkins of Baltimore Maryland had come into the possession of a Milly Winder, a mulatto woman who had become his property through his father's estate in 1817. Milly Winder had given birth that same year to a mulatto female child whose father had been a white man.

There was a long pause then, by Mr. Swift, who clearly must have known that I was born in 1817, but he would need more than that to convince the jury that I belonged to Mr. Aitkins, or at least I prayed such, and watched quietly as everyone seemed to eyeball me from head to toe during the staged pause by Mr. Swift.

Two years after the birth of said child, who was called Emily, Milly Winder was emancipated by Mr. Aitkins, but her child was not included in the emancipation document. Milly left Emily to live in the demandant's home. Said child did indeed live in the demandant's home, the home of Mr. Aitkins, until July of 1825. Then she disappeared. All traces of her existence were gone.

Well, that proves it then, I thought. I couldn't possibly be Emily Winder, I've lived in Philadelphia with my family since I was two. I sat there silently, instantly relieved. I've been in Philadelphia since 1819 or 1820. Certainly no later than 1821? 22? I realized that I didn't really know exactly when I'd moved into the Gilmore home. I just always had. Had I been two, three, four years old when I had arrived. I honestly could not say with certainty, but surely I called Philadelphia home long before 1825. It's funny, you think you know yourself until your memories are put to the test.

Emily Winder's master, Robert Aitkins, advertised for her recovery in the Baltimore Commercial Chronicle of August 27, 1825, Swift continued, then held up for evidence a certified copy of the advertisement that had been run ten years before for the girl named Emily, who had a reward offered for her recovery.

I wondered what the reward was that Maria Congo had received from these evil men with hate in their hearts for her betrayal to my family.

Mr. Aitkins relinquished his search for the girl, Emily, after several months. Then recently, an old black woman, Maria Congo, Swift said, pointing in her direction, contacted my client, Mr. Aitkins, and told him where the child Emily he was looking for was living. She said that Emily was in Philadelphia and that she was now going by the name Mary Gilmore, who works at the Bakery and Confectionary shop owned by Jacob Gilmore on the corner of South Sixth Street near to Spruce Street in the city.

Mr. Aitkins traveled then to Philadelphia with several witnesses.

On the day of his arrival he saw the girl through the window of the bake shop, but not being able to get a good glimpse of her he returned the next morning under the pretense of a purchase of some cakes, but as the girl was nowhere to be seen, Mr. Aitkins left without the cakes and without paying, pretending to have forgotten his money. He said that since returning to Philadelphia he had himself seen Milly in the city. He gave the judge a certified copy of

Mr. Aitkins' father's will, which transferred ownership of Milly Winder to Mr. Aitkins. He was then dismissed.

How could I have not recognized him, I screamed at myself in my head. He was the man who'd left the shop without a receipt. That had been when my father had me stop wearing my locket. My father must have sensed his treachery. How could I have gone against my father's wishes. Why had I disobeyed him. If I got out of this mess, I would never disobey my father again. Only now it may be too late for such promises I feared.

Maria Congo was sworn in next. I felt a stab of bitter hatred in my heart as she scowled at my father from the witness stand. She told the judge that for the past twelve years she had seen Milly Winder make frequent visits to my father's house and shop. I wished I knew who she was referring to. Who was this Milly Winder? All my life people of every color skin frequented my father's bakery, blacks, withies, mulattos. Not one stood out as a woman who could have been my mother. Wouldn't I have known? Sensed something, anything if my real mother had walked into the bakery? I wished I knew what the truth really was. I wished I knew who I was.

The case was adjourned until the next day at ten o'clock. Another long dark night lay ahead of me. I hadn't expected the trial to go on for so long. I had thought my innocence would be far easier to prove. But how could I prove who I wasn't when I didn't know who I was. How could I prove I was not Emily Winder, when in truth, I myself did not know the secrets of my past. I did not even know for myself who I was.

That night none of us could eat our evening meal. Father was scheduled to take the stand the next morning to testify on my behalf and we could tell he was unnerved by the very thought of it.

If he knew that I was a runaway slave, why had he never told ma as much. I remembered what my father had told me over the years. About how the ol' broken angel had brought me to them. Now as he practiced what he was going to say on the witness stand with my brother Jacob, I discovered that that ol' broken angel was no angel at all. She was an ol' white Irish woman, a drunkard, who used to come with me to the bakery sometime prior to 1819 to get stale cakes and scraps that were going to be thrown away. Father said I couldn't have been more than three or four years old and the white woman had said that I was her daughter. She'd told my parents that her husband had been absconded and that she'd been left to raise me all by herself. Every day she'd come into the bakery a little more broken down by the liquor. Until one day she'd asked if my father would take me in. Father didn't like the way the woman looked or how she handled me, and he knew that she wasn't long for this world, and so he and my mother had taken me in, legally adopted me, schooled me, raised me as their own, loved me, he said with what seemed to be a whimper. I'd never seen my father cry before that moment. This trial was beating him down.

Last he'd heard, my father said, was that the poor old woman had died from the drink in a hospital in Philadelphia. My ol' broken angel was an old Irish drunkard, what other secrets from my past would come up at tomorrow's trial? And how could I have been three or four in 1819. Surely, my father had his dates mixed up, but I didn't want to confound the situation any more than it was and I trusted my father to say and do the right things -- still there were many questions that I needed answered when this was over.

With great difficulty we made our way to the court house the next morning. The riots in the city had started up again in full force and there was some question over whether the trial would be able to proceed as planned.

My father was sworn in and testified before the judge that he had never in his life heard of a Milly Winder. He relayed the story of the drunken Irish woman, that I myself had just heard for the first time the night before. Father testified that he didn't even know the old woman's name. But he did know Maria Congo, and he told the judge how on many occasions he had caught her red handed, stealing money and goods from our bakery and our house. He thought that Maria Congo was saying these things now, these lies out of spite, because my father had threatened to have her arrested if she came in our shop again.

My father also said that he remembered the man coming in our shop for some cakes. The man had told my father that he couldn't read or write and that's why he'd wanted a receipt and why he'd sent me to go next door for a receipt. If the man lied about not being able to read or write, what else might he lie about my father said. He looked nervous as he made these accusations against the white man in the court room, the man claiming to own me as his property. I could see in my father's eyes that he wished this man dead.

Suddenly, the door to the court room burst open and a man with a wild and crazed look upon his face announced to the court room that the riots had gotten out of control and that two of the witnesses for the demandant, Mr. Aitkins had been severely injured. I thought they were doing this for affect, but still the court room exploded in a frenzy and the judge started hammering his gavel down upon his desk, crying, "Order, order in the court!"

The trial was postponed for the next day and was adjourned until Monday, June 29th, almost two full weeks away! I wanted to scream, "No, no, no more. Let's end this now!" but I was helpless, a pawn in this wicked game that evil men play. All I could do now was wait, wait and see what happened. I went to stand near my father's side, helping him down from the witness stand and out through the throngs of people outside the court house.

My brother Jacob grabbed me by my wrist, still torn up from the shackles I'd worn just days before. He instructed me to follow him, and making a human chain, Jacob, my father, and I made our way through the crowds back to our house.

In difficult times there is nothing like family to make you strong.

Over the next few weeks, the news of my trial spread like wild fire throughout the country. In truth, no one knew what to make of me. I wasn't sure at all what to make of myself. One morning while my father was making breakfast, I asked him, "Pa, am I black or am I white?" I think I startled him with my candor, because he didn't reply at first. There was a large mixing bowl of eggs beside him on the counter from the woman who kept chickens down the street. She had many different types of chickens. Some l aid brown eggs, some laid white eggs.

My father took up a brown egg in his left hand and a white egg in his right hand and cracked them open at the same time into another mixing bowl.

You could not tell which yolk had come from which shell. They were the same. He spoke not a single word, but stared deeply into my soul. I think that this was my father's way of telling me that he loved me.

I had a great deal of time to think over those next two weeks. One night I overheard my father talking with a woman downstairs in the bakery.

"No, no, I can't not now," father was saying over and over again. I came out onto the landing and peeked through a knot hole in the wood to the kitchen below. There was my father and a white woman and a small black child holding a cookie in a tiny fist. The woman wanted to leave the child with my father for just a few days she said. She clearly had not heard about my case, the case of Mary Gilmore.

I remembered then the many small faces that had come and gone through our home over the years. My mother and father had always helped the needy, mostly children, taking them in, giving them shelter and food until their relatives got back on their feet. Sometimes they were relatives of ours I was told. I guess I had been such a child, but had never seen myself in this light.

My father looked worried. "No, I'd like to help, but I can't, not now. You have to go. Please just go," he implored the woman to leave.

"But the child," the woman said.

"Try this address, my father said, and whispered something into the white woman's ear.

I'd tried to be quiet, but I realized that he'd heard the floor board squeak beneath my feet. I caught his glance directly at me through the tiny hole in the floor. I raced back to my bed, and hoped he wouldn't scold me for eavesdropping. But he did not come in and I lay back and began to count the children who had passed through our house in my mind as one might count sheep. There were so many, so many, many black children that my father had helped over the years. Who were these children my father helped. I'd always understood it to be my father being neighborly, helping others out. Now I lay alone in the darkness, in my current situation, and let my imagination be free -- what if it was something more than neighborly kindness, what if it was the Undergound Railroad that I'd been hearing tell of.

"You spying on me?" my father said, startling me from my thoughts.

I didn't respond.

"Do you have any more of those questions for me, Mary?" he asked me very gently. I think he knew that we had much to talk about. Many secrets to reveal.

He looked surprised when I said, "No, Pa."

Some secrets need never to be revealed if they're done with a pure heart and good intentions. Didn't it say in the Bible, don't let your right hand know what your left is doing.

"Alright then, Mary," he said, "Goodnight."

"Pa," I stopped him, "When I get out of this mess of trouble and am found innocent, I want to help out more in the bakery. I want to help you out. I want to help the people you help."

My father smiled at me in a knowing way, a way I'd never seen him smile at me before. He was proud of me and pleased with what I'd said. I was a part of the secret now.

We said nothing else to one another that night, but we'd come to understand each other more than ever before. And as he was proud of me, I was ultimately more proud of him, my father, Jacob Gilmore, who'd rescued me from a life I can't even begin to imagine.

Samuel visited almost every day of the postponement. We took walks in the park together and read the newspapers together. Sometimes he laughed at how silly some of the headlines were. "The Case of Mary Gilmore" he'd say in a serious voice, sticking out his chin, and squinting his eyes trying to make me laugh, but I never did. There was nothing even remotely humorous about my situation.

"Oh come on, Mary," Samuel said one evening, just before the trial was to start up again. "If you can't laugh at life, it often laughs at you. You're going to get out of this. I just know it."

"I wish I could be so sure as you," I said. "What if I am found guilty, found guilty of being a runaway slave, a fugitive, a felon! Would you still be laughing then, Samuel? Would you even still like me then, Samuel Allen?"

I was more than surprised by his response. It was shocking really, and most unexpected given the circumstances.

"I'd still *love* you then," Samuel said. "Love you, Mary, like I love you now." And then he kissed me.

For the first time in my whole life a had a sense of belonging.

"I love you, too," I said. And I did and he did and we belonged together, Samuel and Mary. We were going to get through this and get married and start a family of our own and work together to help other people like me find their way to freedom.

Maureen Kelly never came by my house to call on me, to see how I was doing, to apologize for her behavior towards me.

A part of me wanted desperately to run next door and see her. I thought of all of the times we'd spent happily playing children's games, oblivious to the terrible things going on all around us. Maybe Maury understood more than I had about such things. She was the one always running into town to see the captured slaves. I must have been living in my own private fantasy world.

Well, my eyes were opened wide now to the slave business weren't they. I saw myself through new eyes. I was no longer a child. I was a woman. A woman who God willing would be found innocent on all charges and marry Samuel Allen.

On Monday, June 29, 1835 the city of Philadelphia was deceptively quiet. Unnaturally quiet. Yesterday at my church, Mother Bethel, the African Methodist Episcopal Church right near our bakery on South Sixth Street, our minister had held my family up in prayer before the whole of the congregation. The church was rumored to be a secret depot of the Underground Railroad, but no one talked about such things openly. I'd felt lifted up by their strength and support. I realized in church seeing my congregation through my new eyes that I was the only white girl in the whole church and I also realized that it did not matter one bit, that I was Jacob Gilmore's daughter and the color of my skin didn't matter to him, he loved me for who I was on the inside. And the people of Philadelphia loved him for this same reason. Why then was I finding it so difficult to stand on my own two feet come Monday morning.

The path was clear all the way to the court house. The silence was deafening on the streets and in the court room. The unusual circumstances of my case had finally dawned on people.

Under the current laws as they were, no one was safe from the treachery of slavery. Anyone, man, woman, or child, regardless of their skin color could be accused of being a fugitive, alleged to be another man's property. All the newspapers of late had taken this bent, and I no longer felt like a spectacle, a curiosity, a mystery to be solved. My case was not simply to determine if I were black or white. My case would set a precedent in the annals of the law. Could a man's right to his freedom be determined solely by the color of his skin? Could it be based on percentages? Did a mulatto have a greater right to freedom than a black and a quadroon an even greater right? If a white person could be found guilty of being a fugitive slave, then how could slavery be upheld under the Constitution as all white men were free? No this case had nothing to do with me anymore, and everything to do with greed, with hate, with the right to own slaves, the right to own other people as property. This frightened the daylights out of me.

I watched as my father took to the witness stand for the second time during this trial. His gait had slowed and he was uneasy on his feet.

Unlike his first appearance in the court, my father was now on the stand for cross-examination by the demandant's counsel.

The questions came at my father in rapid succession and he answered each one without hesitation.

He told of the old woman and her child who was very sickly. He told of how I'd come to his home in 1819 or 1820, but he knew it was not possibly so late as 1824. The child had not been more than three or four years of age, and barely reached to top of the table. He told that on his honor he had never heard before this trial that I was a slave. He had never heard tell of a Milly Winder or an Emily Winder.

George Whitman was then sworn in and testified on behalf of the demandant. He was a wily and cunning looking gentleman who looked very cool in the heat of the court room, and leaned back into the chair on the witness stand with an ease that seemed far too comfortable.

He said that he'd known Robert Aitkin's family for many years. He and his wife knew the child Emily and his wife had seen this same child in 1826 on South Sixth Street in Philadelphia.

The judge would not accept Mr. Whitman's wife's testimony unless she personally gave it under oath herself in the court room. Mrs. Whitman refused to testify, objecting to coming into court and was ordered to be deposed on that same day at another location.

What I couldn't understand was how it was that this wealthy white woman could refuse this judge's order to appear in court. Could I have refused to play this charade anymore if I wanted to and walk away? Not likely I thought.

Robert Aitkin's brother, Doctor James Aitkins was sworn in next. He testified that he too, knew Milly's daughter, Emily, who had been born in 1817. He had not seen her since 1825, ten years back. Her father had been fair born and was long since deceased. He said he saw her now, however, as she was seated directly in front of him as the respondant, Mary Gilmore.

Looking straight at me, with the coldest, cruelest eyes I have ever seen, he said, "I have no doubt of the identity of this young woman, judging as I do of any other fact. This woman is Emily Winder."

I thought my heart would stop beating he said this with such surety.

He went on to state that as a physician and a psychiatrist he could be sure of it, as I was obviously the daughter of a mulatto and a white father.

"I knew as soon as I saw her," he stated quite matter of factly, as if merely swatting off a fly.

The judge asked if he were absolutely positive of his assertion. "Was there any particular mark upon the girl?" the judge prodded, "By which he could positively identify this young woman as Emily Winder?"

"No," Dr. Aitkins said, "There was no mark in particular."

And with that the witness portion of the trial came to a close.

Closing arguments were read and the jury was let out to deliberate.

It was all so sudden, so terribly and horribly sudden.

And now I clung to my father, burying my face in his jacket
which smelled of sugar and molasses and goodness.

"Everything is going to be alright, child. You just wait and see."

But how long would we be made to wait.

Minutes

     Passed

          By

               Like

                    Days.

As we sat outside the court house while the jury made its
deliberations.

"I don't think I can wait much longer," I told my father. "I don't
know what I'll do if they take me away from you."

"Nobody is going to take you away from me, child."

It was getting late in the day and I thought for sure the trial would be adjourned to the following day. People of the jury were going to have to be getting home for their dinners, with their families.

And what about my family? What was going to become of my family if I was found guilty of being a runaway.

My father would be left all alone to run the bakery and confectionary shop. Granny might help out a bit, but she was getting on in years. And what about Samuel and the plans we had made to be together, to have a future -- together?

My brother Jacob squeezed my hand three times tightly. He'd done this since we were small, whenever I was scared or frightened by something, usually something small though, like a bug or a fall.

"You okay?" he asked.

At this point I couldn't be sure whether I was okay or not.

I just nodded.

People from our congregation began to sing a gospel song, raising their voices in a loud crescendo. Anti-abolitionists had seemingly crawled out from whatever rocks that they'd been hiding under during the daylight hours.

A large bird screeched across the sky, high above the tumult and confusion on the streets below. It's wing span was so wide, like that of the pictures of eagles I'd seen. The eagle, the symbol of freedom in these United States. It was a good sign, I told myself.

Just then, the doors to the court house were held wide open and we were summoned back inside to hear the verdict.

It took me ten years to climb the ten stairs to the court room, or at least that's how long each step seemed to take. For my father, it looked like it felt even longer for him.

I just wanted this to be over. I just wanted to be free to live my life again. And to never take that freedom for granted -- not ever again.

Fourth Course: The Proof is in the Pudding

"Bread Pudding: Soak bread crumbs in milk, set aside until cool; add sugar, butter, eggs slightly beaten, salt, and flavoring; bake one hour in buttered pudding-dish in slow oven; serve with Vanilla Sauce."

-- The Boston Cooking School Cook Book by Fannie Merritt Farmer

Philadelphia Ice Cream - thin cream, sweetened, flavored, and frozen

    1 quart thin cream   ¾ cup sugar

           1 ½ tablespoons vanilla

           Mix ingredients, and freeze.

"Ices and other frozen dishes comprise the most popular desserts. Hygienically speaking, they cannot be recommended for the final course of a dinner, as cold mixtures reduce the temperature of the stomach, thus retarding digestion until the normal temperature is again reached. But how cooling, refreshing, and nourishing, when properly taken, and of what inestimable value in the sick room!"

           -- The Boston Cooking School Cook Book by Fannie Merritt Farmer

And just like that, it was over. After three long days of interrogations and witnesses testifying and two long weeks of anticipation while the trial was postponed and the riots ran wild in the streets of Philadelphia, it had all come down to this one moment in time, the final course. I hoped it would not be served cold.

The jury was called back and the judge asked them if they'd arrived at a verdict in the case of Mary Gilmore.

The jury responded that they had. The judge was then handed the piece of paper which held my fate, my freedom. I was thankful that he read the decision without hesitation for affect or to grandstand in anyway.

He simply said, "In the case of Mary Gilmore, the respondant has been found not guilty of being a fugitive slave."

And, just like that, I was Mary Gilmore again. Jacob Gilmore's daughter. Not Emily Winder, Robert Aitkin's slave. I was a free woman -- again.

The judge went on to elaborate upon the jury's decision, stating that as a result of the respondant's being able to prove to the satisfaction of the judge and the jury that I had in fact resided in Pennsylvania for four years prior to when the claimant alleged that his fugitive slave had quit his service, the respondant, Mary Gilmore, was to be immediately discharged.

I can't really recall the order of events from that point on. There arose such a loud clattering of cheers and huzzahs in the court room and the judge began to bang on his desk with his gavel so loudly crying, "Order, order, order in the court!"

I remember my father and brother carrying me out on their shoulders and people dancing in the streets of Philadelphia.

Samuel was cheering the loudest of all. Even now when I look back upon that time in my life, I can't believe it really happened to me. The people from my church and my neighborhood held a grand celebration in my honor that night. The people in attendance were of every color, but the blood that ran through our veins was the same color. We celebrated this unity and prayed for freedom for all people. Prayed for a day that no man would be a slave to another man. When all men would be recognized equal under the laws of our country, regardless of the color of their skin.

I had made many promises over the past few weeks, promises which I planned to keep.

The newspapers around the United States ran many stories on the case of Mary Gilmore.

"This case illustrates the wisdom of the late reformation of our laws regulating the manner in which the claimants shall proceed. And this young girl, as white and free as any in the land would have been hurried away into bitter and hopeless slavery. Many free blacks have thus been carried off this way into slavery," one paper wrote, much like the stories from other newspapers, but I feared the message had been lost. It should not have been the point that if a white person could be so accused, but instead that if any person could be so accused, so mistreated and carried off to be another man's property. Many, many free black men, women, and children had been stolen away in this manner, carried off in this despicable form of legal kidnapping into slavery. Legally kidnapped.

Over the next few weeks I cried so many tears of joy it was as if my eyes, my new eyes through which I now saw the world around me were fountains, bottomless wells of deep running waters.

Samuel asked my father for my hand in marriage, and we began preparations for a September wedding, right before Jacob would go back to school.

Shortly after the trial my father surprised me by giving me back my tiny silver locket.

"M is for Mary," was all he'd said. And I've not take it off since.

Final Course: The Epilogue

"After serving café noir in drawing-room, pass pony of brandy for men, sweet liqueur (Chartreuse, Benedictine, or Parfait d'Amour) for women; then Crème de Menthe for all. Bonbons are passed."

-- The Boston Cooking School Cook Book by Fannie Merritt Farmer

Café Noir

"Café noir may prove beneficial, so great are its stimulating effects."

Now, you the reader might be asking yourself, whether or not Mary Gilmore is black or white, but I ask of you this, "Does the color of a person's skin matter so much? Am I not the same person regardless of how one defines me as either black or white?

I am an old woman now, and when I close my eyes I can go back in time to my days in that bakery and confectionary shop with my father and my mother and my brother Jacob. My family, the people who chose to love me, despite the color of my skin. I can still taste and smell the deliciousness of my father's confections. His Velvet Molasses Candy, Sugared Popped Corn, Butter Taffy, Nougatine Drops, and my favorite his spice cookies.

I lost my father shortly after Samuel and I were married.

He died just before Christmas in 1835 at the far too young age of 51. Almost six months to the day from when the trial was ended and I was proven to be white and thus proven to be free. It was the trial that stole twenty years of my father's life from him, and thus twenty years of time I would have had with my father from me. For that I will always be bitter.

All the newspapers some of which were still running my story, ran his obituary. "Jacob Gilmore, aged 51. The deceased was one of the most respectable colored men of his city. His benevolence was manifested on numerous occasions; and particularly in his undeviating kindness towards the orphan white girl, Mary Gilmore, whose trial excited so much interest in the community during the last summer."

My brother Jacob became a lawyer and fought for the rights of the oppressed all the days of his life.

Samuel and I became conductors on the Underground Railroad and helped to bring thousands of slaves of all complexions to freedom, rescuing thousands from oppression. We served on the Springfield route of the Underground Railroad through Mercer County in Pennsylvania and worked in support of abolition all the days of our lives.

I hope that when and if I am remembered by history, it will be kindly. I tried all of my life to treat all people as equals, and to help those who were not, to find a place where they might so be.

Before I close, I'll try as best as I am able to answer the question which I fear lingers in the mind of the reader. I wouldn't want you to feel cheated after reading my story, the case of Mary Gilmore for so many pages now.

The truth is I look at my reflection every day in the glass and I see only my reflection staring back at me. It is the reflection of an old woman now with a fair complexion, some might call it white, though on sunny days in my youth it would burn red with sunburn.

I never once brought up the question of my race with my father again. After all he'd done on my behalf, how could I? I guess then he carried my secret to the grave with him.

But black or white, I am still Mary Gilmore Allen. And I will affirm my believe with my dying breath that never is there a reason or a right for one man to own another man whether that right be asserted based upon the color of a man's skin, hair, eyes, or teeth for that matter.

I'm glad I've lived long enough to see my children's children grow to be persons of unimpeachable integrity as my father Jacob Gilmore was and that in my lifetime I was witness to the national emancipation of the slaves on January 1, 1863 , but when they look back on my story, I know the question of my heritage will plague a few. "Was she black or was she white?" I can hear them asking still.

The court recognized me as a white girl, and for this I was able to keep the many promises that I had made to myself to help others who themselves were oppressed. Still I'm sure I could have done even more if there had more time. I dream of the day that there will not be a differentiation made between a black America and a white America. I pray each night for a time when there will truly only be a United States of America. I can see that day on the horizon just as clearly as I see my own reflection in the looking glass. One hundred years hence, if I am remembered, let me be remembered as a woman who made a difference, who put a scratch on the surface of the cruelty that the human race is capable of in the way of slavery and exposed it for what it was.

After Dinner Recitals

The following poem appeared in William Lloyd Garrison's

Newspaper, The Liberator on July 18, 1835.

Stanzas

"Written after witnessing the trial of Mary Gilmore, the young and interesting white female whose case has excited so much public sympathy in Philadelphia."

I saw her at the judgment seat

A captive young and fair

And many a heart indignant beat

To see the maiden there.

Each mild and soft and winning grace

Around her features played

While on her sweet and modest face

Was innocence portrayed.

O' what unhappy fate could bring

That tender being there?

To one so gentle, whence could spring

Misfortune so severe?

No guilt was charged against the maid
In action, word, or thought,
Yet there be cruel hands conveyed
To judgment she was brought.

Shame to the age - to manhood shame!
Amidst the free and brave
Boldness could seize and avarice claim
That fair one as a slave!

Was there no virtuous arm of might
When the foul deed was done
In zeal for lovely woman' right
To avenge the injured one?

Ah! No- the cold unfeeling law
Must hear the ruffian's plea--
Justice at length th'injustice saw,
And bade the maid go free.

Yet wields that law no righteous rod

To check the bold offence,

Th'unhallowed plunderer roams abroad

To pray on innocence.

Thus they in human flesh who trade

Nor hue nor sex will spare

The happiest homes they oft invade

And scatter ruin there.

Alas! Tis thus in Freedom's land

We feel oppression's sway.

Thy genius, Slavery, gives command--

Our lot is to obey.

--Virginius

July 1835

Glossary

Fugitive Slave Act of 1793 was a law which was written with the intention of enforcing an article of the Constitution of the time which required the return of runaway slaves. It sought to force the authorities in the free states to return fugitive slaves to their masters. Some Northern states passed "personal liberty laws" which mandated a jury trial before alleged fugitive slaves could be moved. Otherwise, they feared free blacks could be kidnapped into slavery. Other states forbade the use of local jails or the assistance of state officials in the arrest or return of such fugitives. In some cases, juries simply refused to convict individuals who had been indicted under the Federal law.

Fugitive Slave Act of 1850 was passed by the Congress as part of the Compromise of 1850. This was one of the most controversial acts of the 1850 compromise. It declared that all runaway slaves be brought back to their masters.

The Reverse Underground Railroad is the term used for the historical practice of the kidnapping of African Americans from the free states and the transportation of these free people into the South for sale into slavery as slaves. The term implies the opposite of the Underground Railroad, the network of the anti-slavery movements and abolitionists in the United States who helped to free captive African Americans who were slaves and bring them to the North and freedom.

Fugitive Slave Act of 1793

An Act respecting fugitives from justice, and persons escaping from the service of their masters.

Be it enacted, &c., That, whenever the Executive authority of any State in the Union, or of either of the Territories Northwest or South of the river Ohio, shall demand any person as a fugitive from justice, of the Executive authority of any such State or Territory to which such person shall have fled, and shall moreover produce the copy of an indictment found, or an affidavit made before a magistrate of any State or Territory as aforesaid, charging the person so demanded with having committed treason, felony, or other crime, certified as authentic by the Governor or Chief Magistrate of the State or Territory from whence the person so charged fled, it shall be the duty of the executive authority of the State or Territory to which such person shall have fled, to cause him or her arrest to be given to the Executive authority making such demand, or to the agent when he shall appear; but, if no such agent shall appear within six months from the time of the arrest, the prisoner may be discharged: and all costs or expenses incurred in the apprehending, securing, and transmitting such fugitive to the State or Territory making such demand, shall be paid by such State or Territory.

SEC. 2. *And be it further enacted*, That any agent appointed as aforesaid, who shall receive the fugitive into his custody, shall be empowered to transport him or her to the State or Territory from which he or she shall have fled. And if any person or persons shall, by force, set at liberty, or rescue the fugitive from such agent while transporting, as aforesaid, the person or persons so offending shall, on conviction, be fined not exceeding five hundred dollars, and be imprisoned not exceeding one year.

SEC. 3. *And be it also enacted*, That when a person held to labor in any of the United States, or in either of the Territories on the Northwest or South of the river Ohio, under the laws thereof, shall escape into any other part of the said States or Territory, the person to whom such labor or service may be due, his agent or attorney, is hereby empowered to seize or arrest such fugitive from labor, and to take him or her before any Judge of the Circuit or District Courts of the United States, residing or being within the State, or before any magistrate of a county, city, or town corporate, wherein such seizure or arrest shall be made, and upon proof to the satisfaction of such Judge or magistrate, either by oral testimony or affidavit taken before and certified by a magistrate of any such State or Territory, that the person so seized or arrested, doth, under the laws of the State or Territory from which he or she fled, owe service or labor to the person claiming him or her, it shall be the duty of such Judge or magistrate to give a certificate thereof to such claimant, his agent, or attorney, which shall be sufficient warrant for removing the said fugitive from labor to the State or Territory from which he or she fled.

SEC. 4. *And be it further enacted*, That any person who shall knowingly and willingly obstruct or hinder such claimant, his agent, or attorney, in so seizing or arresting such fugitive from labor, or shall rescue such fugitive from such claimant, his agent or attorney, when so arrested pursuant to the authority herein given and declared; or shall harbor or conceal such person after notice that he or she was a fugitive from labor, as aforesaid, shall, for either of the said offences, forfeit and pay the sum of five hundred dollars. Which penalty may be recovered by and for the benefit of such claimant, by action of debt, in any Court proper to try the same, saving moreover to the person claiming such labor or service his right of action for or on account of the said injuries, or either of them.

Approved [signed into law by President George Washington], February 12, 1793.

Fugitive Slave Act of 1850

Be it enacted by the Senate and House of Representatives of the United States of America in Congress assembled, That the persons who have been, or may hereafter be, appointed commissioners, in virtue of any act of Congress, by the Circuit Courts of the United States, and Who, in consequence of such appointment, are authorized to exercise the powers that any justice of the peace, or other magistrate of any of the United States, may exercise in respect to offenders for any crime or offense against the United States, by arresting, imprisoning, or bailing the same under and by the virtue of the thirty-third section of the act of the twenty-fourth of September seventeen hundred and eighty-nine, entitled "An Act to establish the judicial courts of the United States" shall be, and are hereby, authorized and required to exercise and discharge all the powers and duties conferred by this act.

§ 2. And be it further enacted, That the Superior Court of each organized Territory of the United States shall have the same power to appoint commissioners to take acknowledgments of bail and affidavits, and to take depositions of witnesses in civil causes, which is now possessed by the Circuit Court of the United States; and all commissioners who shall hereafter be appointed for such purposes by the Superior Court of any organized Territory of the United States, shall possess all the powers, and exercise all the duties, conferred by law upon the commissioners appointed by the Circuit Courts of the United States for similar purposes, and shall moreover exercise and discharge all the powers and duties conferred by this act.

§ 3. And be it further enacted, That the Circuit Courts of the United States shall from time to time enlarge the number of the commissioners, with a view to afford reasonable facilities to reclaim fugitives from labor, and to the prompt discharge of the duties imposed by this act.

§ 4. And be it further enacted, That the commissioners above named shall have concurrent jurisdiction with the judges of the Circuit and District Courts of the United States, in their respective circuits and districts within the several States, and the judges of the Superior Courts of the Territories, severally and collectively, in term-time and vacation; shall grant certificates to such claimants, upon satisfactory proof being made, with authority to take and remove such fugitives from service or labor, under the restrictions herein contained, to the State or Territory from which such persons may have escaped or fled.

§ 5. And be it further enacted, That it shall be the duty of all marshals and deputy marshals to obey and execute all warrants and precepts issued under the provisions of this act, when to them directed; and should any marshal or deputy marshal refuse to receive such warrant, or other process, when tendered, or to use all proper means diligently to execute the same, he shall, on conviction thereof, be fined in the sum of one thousand dollars, to the use of such claimant, on the motion of such claimant, by the Circuit or District Court for the district of such marshal; and after arrest of such fugitive, by such marshal or his deputy, or whilst at any time in his custody under the provisions of this act, should such fugitive escape, whether with or without the assent of such marshal or his deputy, such marshal shall be liable, on his official bond, to be prosecuted for the benefit of such claimant, for the full value of the service or labor of said fugitive in the State, Territory, or District whence he escaped: and the better to enable the said commissioners, when thus appointed, to execute their duties faithfully and efficiently, in conformity with the requirements of the Constitution of the United States and of this act, they are hereby authorized and empowered, within their counties respectively, to appoint, in writing under their hands, any one or more suitable persons, from time to time, to execute all such warrants and other process as may be issued by them in the lawful performance of their respective duties; with authority to such commissioners, or the persons to be appointed by them, to execute process as aforesaid, to summon and call to their aid the bystanders, or posse comitatus of the proper county, when necessary to ensure a faithful observance of the clause of the Constitution referred to, in conformity with the provisions of this act; and all good citizens are hereby commanded to aid and assist in the prompt and efficient execution of this law, whenever their services may be required, as aforesaid, for that purpose; and said warrants shall run, and be executed by said officers, any where in the State within which they are issued.

§ 6. And be it further enacted, That when a person held to service or labor in any State or Territory of the United States, has heretofore or shall hereafter escape into another State or Territory of the United

States, the person or persons to whom such service or labor may be due, or his, her, or their agent or attorney, duly authorized, by power of attorney, in writing, acknowledged and certified under the seal of some legal officer or court of the State or Territory in which the same may be executed, may pursue and reclaim such fugitive person, either by procuring a warrant from some one of the courts, judges, or commissioners aforesaid, of the proper circuit, district, or county, for the apprehension of such fugitive from service or labor, or by seizing and arresting such fugitive, where the same can be done without process, and by taking, or causing such person to be taken, forthwith before such court, judge, or commissioner, whose duty it shall be to hear and determine the case of such claimant in a summary manner; and upon satisfactory proof being made, by deposition or affidavit, in writing, to be taken and certified by such court, judge, or commissioner, or by other satisfactory testimony, duly taken and certified by some court, magistrate, justice of the peace, or other legal officer authorized to administer an oath and take depositions under the laws of the State or Territory from which such person owing service or labor may have escaped, with a certificate of such magistracy or other authority, as aforesaid, with the seal of the proper court or officer thereto attached, which seal shall be sufficient

to establish the competency of the proof, and with proof, also by

affidavit, of the identity of the person whose service or labor is

claimed to be due as aforesaid, that the person so arrested does in

fact owe service or labor to the person or persons claiming him or

her, in the State or Territory from which such fugitive may have

escaped as aforesaid, and that said person escaped, to make out and

deliver to such claimant, his or her agent or attorney, a certificate

setting forth the substantial facts as to the service or labor due from

such fugitive to the claimant, and of his or her escape from the State

or Territory in which he or she was arrested, with authority to such

claimant, or his or her agent or attorney, to use such reasonable force

and restraint as may be necessary, under the circumstances of the

case, to take and remove such fugitive person back to the State or

Territory whence he or she may have escaped as aforesaid. In no

trial or hearing under this act shall the testimony of such alleged

fugitive be admitted in evidence; and the certificates in this and the

first [fourth] section mentioned, shall be conclusive of the right of

the person or persons in whose favor granted, to remove such

fugitive to the State or Territory from which he escaped, and shall prevent all molestation of such person or persons by any process issued by any court, judge, magistrate, or other person whomsoever.

§ 7. And be it further enacted, That any person who shall knowingly and willingly obstruct, hinder, or prevent such claimant, his agent or attorney, or any person or persons lawfully assisting him, her, or them, from arresting such a fugitive from service or labor, either with or without process as aforesaid, or shall rescue, or attempt to rescue, such fugitive from service or labor, from the custody of such claimant, his or her agent or attorney, or other person or persons lawfully assisting as aforesaid, when so arrested, pursuant to the authority herein given and declared; or shall aid, abet, or assist such person so owing service or labor as aforesaid, directly or indirectly, to escape from such claimant, his agent or attorney, or other person or persons legally authorized as aforesaid; or shall harbor or conceal such fugitive, so as to prevent the discovery and arrest of such person, after notice or knowledge of the fact that such person was a fugitive from service or labor as aforesaid, shall, for either of said offences, be subject to a fine not exceeding one thousand dollars, and imprisonment not exceeding six months, by indictment and conviction before the District Court of the United States for the district in which such offence may have been committed, or before the proper court of criminal jurisdiction, if committed within any one of the organized Territories of the United States; and shall moreover forfeit and pay, by way of civil damages to the party injured by such illegal conduct, the sum of one thousand dollars for each fugitive so lost as aforesaid, to be recovered by action of debt, in any of the District or Territorial Courts aforesaid, within whose jurisdiction the said offence may have been committed.

§ 8. And be it further enacted, That the marshals, their deputies, and the clerks of the said District and Territorial Courts, shall be paid, for their services, the like fees as may be allowed for similar services in other cases; and where such services are rendered exclusively in the arrest, custody, and delivery of the fugitive to the claimant, his or her agent or attorney, or where such supposed fugitive may be discharged out of custody for the want of sufficient proof as aforesaid, then such fees are to be paid in whole by such claimant, his or her agent or attorney; and in all cases where the proceedings are before a commissioner, he shall be entitled to a fee of ten dollars in full for his services in each case, upon the delivery of the said certificate to the claimant, his agent or attorney; or a fee of five dollars in cases where the proof shall not, in the opinion of such commissioner, warrant such certificate and delivery, inclusive of all services incident to such arrest and examination, to be paid, in either case, by the claimant, his or her agent or attorney. The person or persons authorized to execute the process to be issued by such commissioner for the arrest and detention of fugitives from service or labor as aforesaid, shall also be entitled to a fee of five dollars each for each person he or they may arrest, and take before any commissioner as aforesaid, at the instance and request of such claimant, with such other fees as may be deemed reasonable by such commissioner for such other additional services as may be necessarily performed by him or them; such as attending at the examination, keeping the fugitive in custody, and providing him with food and lodging during his detention, and until the final determination of such commissioners; and, in general, for performing such other duties as may be required by such claimant, his or her attorney or agent, or commissioner in the premises, such fees to be made up in conformity with the fees usually charged by the officers of the courts of justice within the proper district or county, as near as may be practicable, and paid by such claimants, their agents or attorneys, whether such supposed fugitives from service or labor be ordered to be delivered to such claimant by the final determination of such commissioner or not.

§ 9. And be it further enacted, That, upon affidavit made by the claimant of such fugitive, his agent or attorney, after such certificate has been issued, that he has reason to apprehend that such fugitive will he rescued by force from his or their possession before he can be taken beyond the limits of the State in which the arrest is made, it shall be the duty of the officer making the arrest to retain such fugitive in his custody, and to remove him to the State whence he fled, and there to deliver him to said claimant, his agent, or attorney. And to this end, the officer aforesaid is hereby authorized and required to employ so many persons as he may deem necessary to overcome such force, and to retain them in his service so long as circumstances may require. The said officer and his assistants, while so employed, to receive the same compensation, and to be allowed the same expenses, as are now allowed by law for transportation of criminals, to be certified by the judge of the district within which the arrest is made, and paid out of the treasury of the United States.

§ 10. And be it further enacted, That when any person held to service or labor in any State or Territory, or in the District of Columbia, shall escape therefrom, the party to whom such service or labor shall be due, his, her, or their agent or attorney, may apply to any court of record therein, or judge thereof in vacation, and make satisfactory proof to such court, or judge in vacation, of the escape aforesaid, and that the person escaping owed service or labor to such party. Whereupon the court shall cause a record to be made of the matters so proved, and also a general description of the person so escaping, with such convenient certainty as may be; and a transcript of such record, authenticated by the attestation of the clerk and of the seal of the said court, being produced in any other State, Territory, or district in which the person so escaping may be found, and being exhibited to any judge, commissioner, or other office, authorized by the law of the United States to cause persons escaping from service or labor to be delivered up, shall be held and taken to be full and conclusive evidence of the fact of escape, and that the service or labor of the person escaping is due to the party in such record mentioned. And upon the production by the said party of other and further evidence if necessary, either oral or by affidavit, in addition to what is contained in the said record of the identity of the person escaping, he or she shall be delivered up to the claimant, And the said court, commissioner, judge, or other person authorized by this act to grant certificates to claimants or fugitives, shall, upon the production of the record and other evidences aforesaid, grant to such claimant a certificate of his right to take any such person identified and proved to be owing service or labor as aforesaid, which certificate shall authorize such claimant to seize or arrest and transport such person to the State or Territory from which he escaped: Provided, That nothing herein contained shall be construed as requiring the production of a transcript of such record as evidence as aforesaid. But in its absence the claim shall be heard and determined upon other satisfactory proofs, competent in law.

Approved, September 18, 1850.

The End

Printed in Great Britain
by Amazon